How To Successfully Day Trade Options on Robinhood

By Michael Henderson

Table of Contents

RISK WARNING

How To Successfully Day Trade Options on Robinhood offers general trading advice that does not take into consideration your own trading experiences, personal objectives and goals, financial means or risk tolerance. If you have any concerns, it is suggested that you seek advice from a professional financial advisor. Keep in mind that past performance is no indication of future results.

Disclaimer

==========

Last updated: August 29, 2023

The information contained in How To Successfully Day Trade Options on Robinhood (the "Book") is for general information purposes only. Michael Henderson (the "Author") assumes no responsibility for errors or omissions in the contents in the Book.

In no event shall Michael Henderson be liable for any special, direct, indirect, consequential, or incidental damages or any damages whatsoever, whether in an action of contract, negligence or other tort, arising out of or in connection with the use of the Book or the contents of the Book. Michael Henderson (the "Author") reserves the right to make additions, deletions, or modification to the contents in the Book at any time without prior notice.

This book I dedicate to all new children books illustrators who have a passion to see children smile and just need a little extra side money to get the career going.

Note from the author:

I wrote this book to teach people my strategy on how to day trade options. It's a small book because I was unwilling to fill it with unnecessary information. You bought this book to learn my strategy for trading options and that's what I wanted to deliver on. I chiseled the book down so much that I didn't even need to divide it up into chapters. It's broken down into four sections: The basics, risk management, my options day trading strategy and pattern day trade rule. I pray you find this format useful and the information helpful and more importantly profitable.

Your truly,
Michael Henderson

The thing that makes making money a rewarding and joyous activity is that when God blesses you with more than enough of it you can become a blessing to those less fortunate than you. But, in order to do that you must have an understanding that all the money everywhere belongs to God and you're just being steward over the portion he gave you. But this point of view depends on your relationship with the greatest gift God has ever given human society and that's Jesus Christ.

So as I got ready to publish this book I felt it wasn't complete unless I gave you the opportunity to accept Jesus Christ as your Lord and savior. What that means is you believe 2000 years ago Jesus died on the cross for you that you might be saved. This is so important I couldn't ignore it. For me to teach you about day trading and not share Jesus Christ with you in a moment in time that will never happen again between you and I would be wrong on my part being a disciple of Christ.

Furthermore, there is a link between being successful financially and the application of biblical principles about money. In fact, it's been said that Jesus talked more about money than faith and prayer combined. And one of his biggest concerns was not you having money but your relationship with it.

I Timothy 6:10

For the LOVE of money is a ROOT of all kinds of evil. Some people, eager for money, have wandered from the faith and pierced themselves with many griefs.

Jesus even went as far to teach us what to do with money and became angered when we mismanaged it.

Matthew 25: 14-30

Again, it will be like a man going on a journey, who called his servants and entrusted his wealth to them. 15

To one he gave five bags of gold, to another two bags, and to another one bag,[a] each according to his ability. Then he went on his journey. 16 The man who had received five bags of gold went at once and put his money to work and gained five bags more.17 So also, the one with two bags of gold gained two more. 18 But the man who had received one bag went off, dug a hole in the ground and hid his master's money.

19 "After a long time the master of those servants returned and settled accounts with them.20 The man who had received five bags of gold brought the other five. 'Master,' he said, 'you entrusted me with five bags of gold. See, I have gained five more.'

21 "His master replied, 'Well done, good and faithful servant! You have been faithful with a few things; I will put you in charge of many things. Come and share your master's happiness!'

22 "The man with two bags of gold also came. 'Master,' he said, 'you entrusted me with two bags of gold; see, I have gained two more.'

23 "His master replied, 'Well done, good and faithful servant! You have been faithful with a few things; I will put you in charge of many things. Come and share your master's happiness!'

24 "Then the man who had received one bag of gold came. 'Master,' he said, 'I knew that you are a hard

man, harvesting where you have not sown and gathering where you have not scattered seed. 25 So I was afraid and went out and hid your gold in the ground. See, here is what belongs to you.'

26 "His master replied, 'You wicked, lazy servant! So you knew that I harvest where I have not sown and gather where I have not scattered seed?27 Well then, you should have put my money on deposit with the bankers, so that when I returned I would have received it back with interest.

28 "'So take the bag of gold from him and give it to the one who has ten bags. 29 For whoever has will be given more, and they will have an abundance. Whoever does not have, even what they have will be taken from them. 30 And throw that worthless servant outside, into the darkness, where there will be weeping and gnashing of teeth.'

So before we go any further, let's get you into right relationship with God so he can help you get into a right relationship with money. The bible says if you confess with your mouth the Lord Jesus and believe in your heart that God has raised Him from the dead, you will be saved. Please repeat this aloud:

9 that if you confess with your mouth the Lord Jesus and believe in your heart that God has raised Him from the dead, you will be saved.

Father God, I am a sinner in need of savior. I believe you died on the cross for me, so I confess with my mouth that you are Lord Jesus, and I believe in my heart that you rose from the dead, and for that I shall be saved…Amen.

Grace and Peace

SECTION ONE: DAY TRADING BASICS

What is day trading?

Day trading is the buying and selling of shares of a stock intraday (same day). For example, if a person buys 10 shares of XYZ company for $10.00 a share at 10 am on January 20, 2023 and sell those 10 shares at 11:00 am on January 20,

2023 regardless if price went above $10.00 or below $10.00 during that 60 minutes this is considered a day trade. If the person were to sell those shares after January 20, 2023 regardless of the time the trade would no longer be considered a day trade. This information is important because the SEC (Security Exchange Commission), the entity that regulates trading, has specific rules for day trading versus long term investing and everyone who day trades has to abide by them.

Can You Day Trade?

The answer to this question is yes. But, a more relevant question to ask is should you day trade? And the answer to that is maybe. Successful day trading requires a unique set of skills and disciplines not native to the average person and until these skills and disciplines are developed then **no, you should not day trade**.

SECTIONS TWO: RISK MANAGEMENT

Back in 2018 I wrote a book about day trading on the platform called Robinhood and in that book I go into detail and explain the basics of day trading. So to avoid being redundant I'll leave that information out. Now If you really want to learn the basics of day trading then go and get my first book *How To Successfully Day Trade on Robinhood*. It's only $8 if you get the ebook. There's also the university of YouTube as well and you can't beat that.

Please don't be upset but the reason I prefer to skip the basics is because I am not a fan of books that go through so much unnecessary information before telling you what you bought the book for in the first place. So I can't be against something and turn around and do it myself. You're reading this book to learn the strategy I use almost everyday to generate hundreds of dollars weekly from day trading options so let's get into it.

Before we get into the nitty-gritty **I MUST** go over the most important thing about day trading and no, it's not consistently making money. The most important topic when discussing day trading: **RISK MANAGEMENT**. This I cannot skip.

Of all the topics discussed within this book, understanding risk management and the role it plays in you becoming a successful day trader is hands down the most important. Within day trading risk takes on many forms and you must familiarize yourself with each one.

Exposure Risk - This is the length of time you're within a trade. Day traders normally don't stay in positions no longer than five minutes or even less. They get in then get out, hopefully taking profits with them. But with the strategy I use day trading options you have some leeway because options come with expiration dates which could be to your benefit if a trade unexpectedly doesn't go in your favor. More on this later.

In my experience the best trades usually go in the direction you expect them to go (whether that's up for call positions or down for put positions) immediately after you enter them.

Especially if you had a very good entry. If that doesn't happen there's no need to keep holding the trade--GET OUT! Then look for another set up.

- Why do traders hold onto losing trades? Remember when I said *Successful day trading requires a unique set of skills and disciplines not native to the average person* one of those skills is recognizing a loss, letting go of the trade and not getting emotionally attached to the trade. What makes letting go even more difficult is the pattern day trading rule which only **allows 3 day trades within a 5 day rolling period.** If you're in a losing trade and it is the last trade you can take until the 5 days pass by, it makes it even harder to let go of the losing trade. This is when you get into the mindfulness and psychology of day trading because now you are irrational, emotional, not thinking clearly, hoping and praying the trade reverses and gives you back your money. If you want to be successful at day trading options **you can not play that game**. Let the trade go and move on to the next one. Furthermore, I'm going to show a way to get around that nasty pattern day trade rule. (More of this later)

- Why should you let go of losing trades fast or how we say in the day trading world; cut your loss?

This will be understood better if I give you an example. Let's say you jump into a trade with a hundred shares and the stock unexpectedly doesn't go in your favor. The stock drops 0.50 cents causing you to have an unrealized loss of $50.00 (100 shares x 0.50 cents = $50.00). Let's also say your daily max loss amount is $50.00. So according to your trading plan this should be the point where you let go of the trade and cut your loss. But instead of cutting the loss you get emotional and hold onto the trade and the stock price falls even deeper and it is $1.75 down from where you originally entered causing you to have an unrealized $175.00 loss. Now the loss is too painful and now you decide to get out of the trade. You're too upset to continue to trade that day so you decide to try again the next day. Now let's say on this day you find another set up that you like and you jump into a trade again. This time the trade goes in your favor and squeezes up $2.00 from where you entered the trade giving an unrealized gain of $200.00 and finally you get out taking your $200.00 profits with you. The hard truth is you did not profit $200.00, you're only up $25.00 because the day before you lost $175.00. But had you cut the loss the day before at your max loss you would be up $150.00 versus $25.00. Moral of the story: CUT YOUR LOSSES there will always be another trade.

Distance between Stop loss vs. Profit Target Risk - This is the gap between the price point where you entered the trade, the price point where you expect the price to go and the price point where you plan to exit the trade if it unexpectedly doesn't go in your favor. The better you are at this the more successful you'll be at trading. **You must have good entry points** (which is another piece to my day trading options strategy that'll go into detail in section three) anticipating the point where the stock will break out because no day trader ever is clairvoyant or psychic enough to capture a stock's entire upward move. And if you are getting in too late you'll be getting in when a stock is on its way down or up for put positions costing you to lose money.

For example: let's say you get into a trade at $55.35 (Price where you entered) and you set for yourself a twenty-five cent profit target of $55.60 (The price point where you expect the price to go and you'll sell your position and take your profits). You'll also want to set a stop loss target of twenty-five cents at $55.05 (price point where you plan to exit the trade, sell your position and take the loss if it unexpectedly doesn't go in your favor). This distance between your stop loss and profit target is the distance between stop loss vs. profit target risk.

Talking about profit and stop loss makes this a good place to mention profit loss ratios. This is your average winners against your average losers. In order to be a profitable day trader you need to consistently trade with a positive profit loss ratio. Most successful traders aim for a 2:1 profit loss ratio. In other words, whatever they are willing to risk in loss, they stand to double that if they profit. They'll risk $0.10 in order to make $0.20.

Using the example from above, let's say you get into a trade at $55.35 (The price where you entered the trade) but this time instead of setting a twenty-five cent profit target of $55.60, you set a sixty-five cents profit target of $56.00, (The price point where you expect the price to go) and a thirty cents stop loss at $55.05 (The price where you'll at sell at if the trade goes against you). The reason for this is to operate at a 2:1 profit loss ratio. Risking one dollar to make two.

What you don't want to do is consistently trade at a negative profit loss ratio like 1:2, risking two dollars to make one dollar.

To help you see the importance of profit loss ratio here's some stats to remember:

2:1 Profit loss ratio = 33% accuracy is break even
   You have to be right about your trades 33% of the time to break even

1:1 Profit loss ratio = 50% accuracy is break even
   You have to be right about your trades 50% of the time to break even

1:2 Profit loss ratio = 66% accuracy is break even
   You have to be right about your trades 66% of the time to break even.

Max Loss - Your max loss is the maximum amount of money you're willing to lose in a single day before you stop trading for that day. **Always have a max loss**.

For example: If your max loss is $1000/day once you lose $1000, regardless how many trades you've taken or didn't take yet and whether its 9:31am and the trading day just started or its 3:30 pm and its close to the end of the trading day, YOUR DAY IS DONE. Rest your emotions, take a step back and clear your head. But, I'll be the first to tell you that this is easier said than done.

SECTION THREE: MY DAY TRADING OPTION STRATEGY

Here's how I day trade options:

If you are familiar with day trading don't let the word options scare you. Just as you take a long position when you buy shares of a stock in hopes that the stock goes up in price or a short position when you sell shares of a stock in hopes that the stock price goes down the same is true when with options contracts. **Traders who are bullish on a stock hoping the stock price increases take *call* positions and traders who are bearish on a stock hoping the price decreases take *put* positions. See S-3: Fig1**

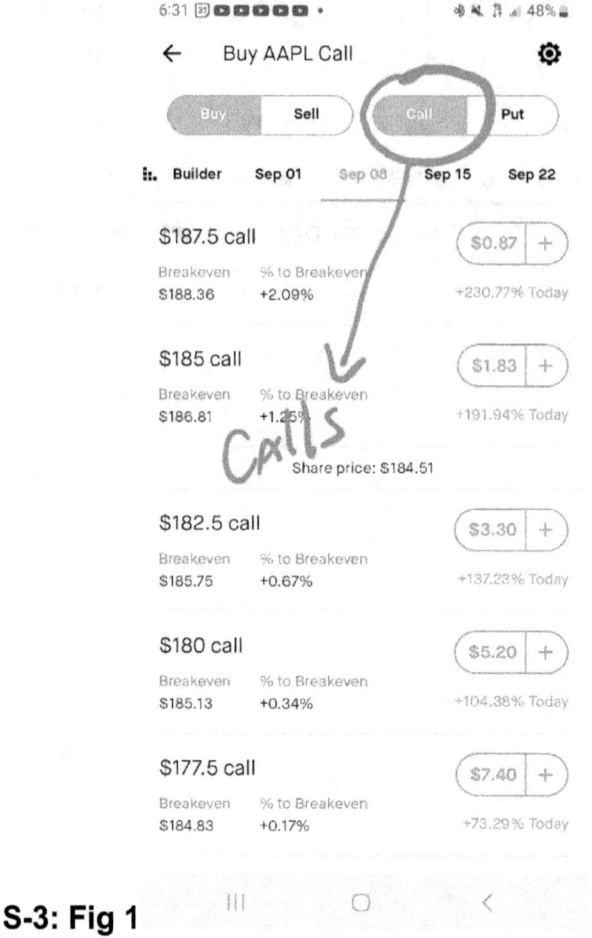

S-3: Fig 1

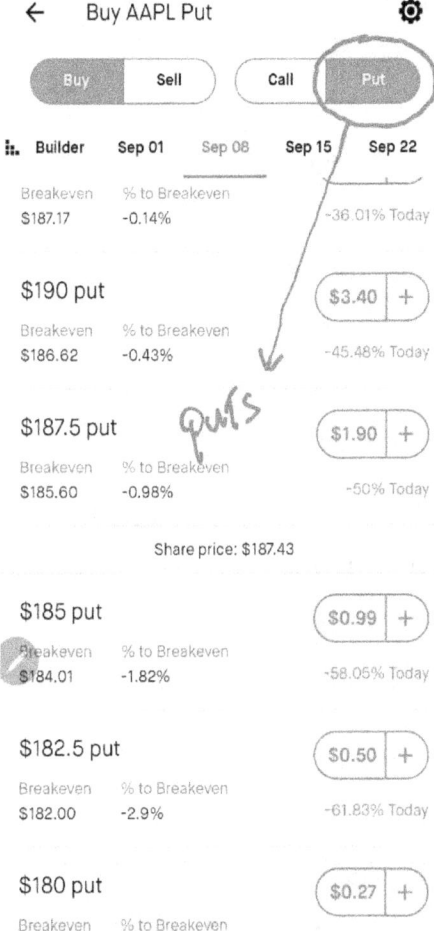

| Buy | Sell | | Call | Put |

| ⠿ Builder | Sep 01 | Sep 08 | Sep 15 | Sep 22 |

| Breakeven | % to Breakeven | | |
| $187.17 | -0.14% | | -36.01% Today |

$190 put $3.40   +

| Breakeven | % to Breakeven | | |
| $186.62 | -0.43% | | -45.48% Today |

$187.5 put   *puts* $1.90   +

| Breakeven | % to Breakeven | | |
| $185.60 | -0.98% | | -50% Today |

Share price: $187.43

$185 put $0.99   +

| Breakeven | % to Breakeven | | |
| $184.01 | -1.82% | | -58.05% Today |

$182.5 put $0.50   +

| Breakeven | % to Breakeven | | |
| $182.00 | -2.9% | | -61.83% Today |

$180 put $0.27   +

| Breakeven | % to Breakeven | | |

The positions I trade mostly are call positions. It is my belief that the stock market has a long bais versus a short bias so I've always felt more confident in hoping stock prices are going to go up versus going down and my trade results as it pertains to my strategy prove me right. I'm not saying a trader can't make money taking short or put positions but I don't unless I'm trading vertical spreads where I know how much I stand to lose before I take trades or there is economic news that will negatively impact the market causing a downtrend. That's something I cover in another book I wrote titled *How to successfully trade credit and debit spreads for weekly extra income.* I had to learn how to do credit and debit spreads because I couldn't day trade at the time because my wife and I just had a baby and sitting in front of a computer screen watching price movements wasn't going to fly in my house.

First thing first, it should be obvious because the title of this book gives it away but in order to trade my strategy and follow along with me you should be using the trading platform Robinhood which is an app you can download to your mobile device.

I prefer using Robinhood on my mobile device as compared to other trading platforms mobile apps because of the ease of use. The user interface is clean and easy to understand. Once I'm logged into my account I'm quickly able to see how much money
I have available to trade with. See S-3: Fig 2

S-3: Fig 2

I say that because if you're already holding some positions and that portion of the cash is tied up, the Robinhood app shows exactly how much buying power you have.

If you are going to trade my strategy I recommend keeping $1500 or more available in buying power so you can get the best entry points for my strategy and a more profitable delta. (More on entry points later)

How do I find which stocks with options contracts to day trade:

Outside of you building your own stock watching list another thing I like about Robinhood is the preset stock screener they have within the app: Within the app it is called *trending list*

← Search Robinhood...

Trending Lists ⓘ

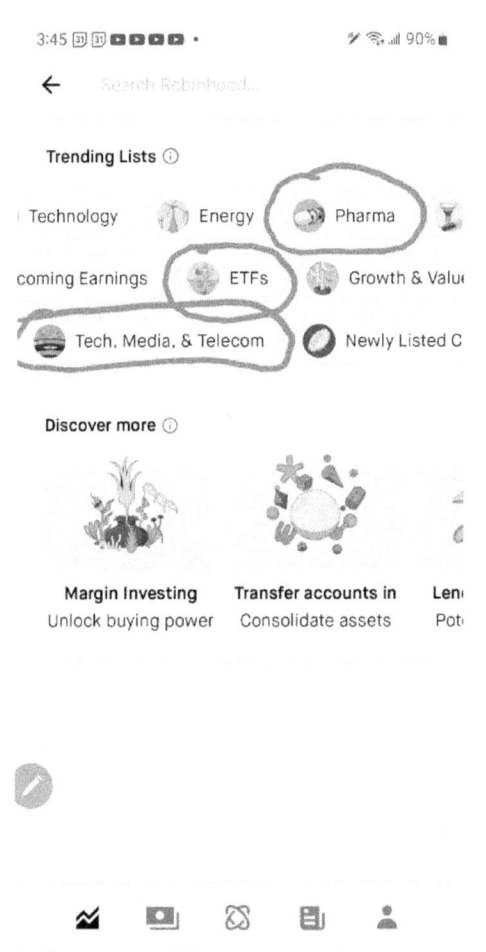

Technology　　🌀 Energy　　🔵 Pharma　　⌛

coming Earnings　　🌀 ETFs　　🔵 Growth & Valu

🔵 Tech, Media, & Telecom　　🔴 Newly Listed C

Discover more ⓘ

Margin Investing　　**Transfer accounts in**　　Len
Unlock buying power　　Consolidate assets　　Pot

S-3 Fig 3

Trending Lists ⓘ

24 Hour Market 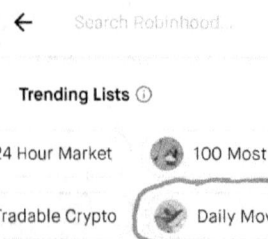 100 Most Popular Tec

Tradable Crypto  Daily Movers Upcomi

IPO Access Altcoins Cannabis

Discover more ⓘ

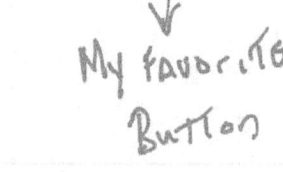

Margin Investing **Transfer accounts in** Len
Unlock buying power Consolidate assets Pot

My fAvoriTG
ButTon

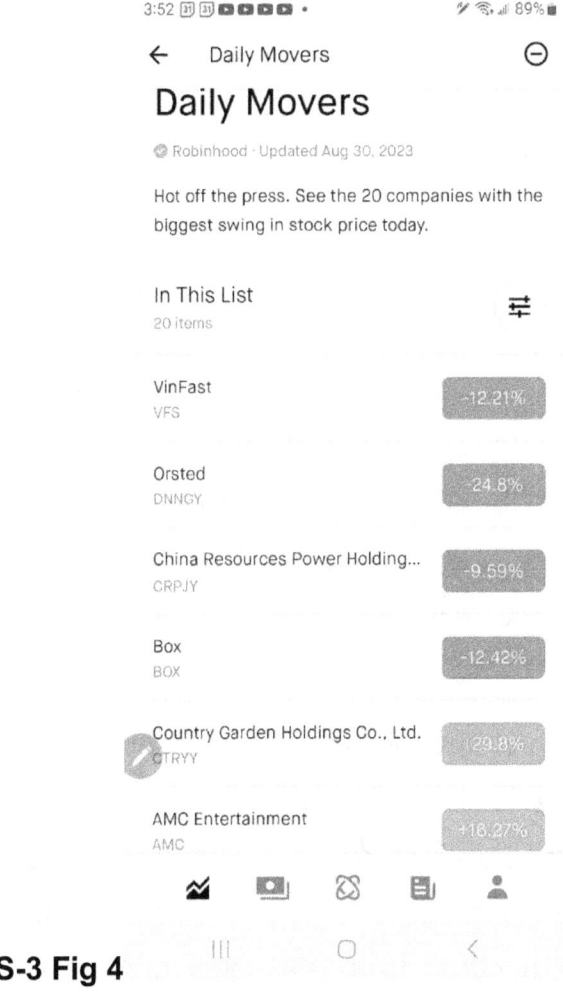

Daily Movers

Robinhood · Updated Aug 30, 2023

Hot off the press. See the 20 companies with the biggest swing in stock price today.

In This List
20 items

VinFast VFS	-12.21%
Orsted DNNGY	-24.8%
China Resources Power Holding... CRPJY	-9.59%
Box BOX	-12.42%
Country Garden Holdings Co., Ltd. CTRYY	29.8%
AMC Entertainment AMC	+18.27%

S-3 Fig 4

For example, if I want trade EFTs I can click on that button and walla ETFs show up. If I want to trade Pharmaceutical stocks, energy stocks, or telecom and media stocks I simply click on those buttons respectively and boom those stocks come up. But since we are discussing day trading, the I button

I look for when I don't see any stocks moving on my own watch list is the daily movers button. This button shows 20 companies with the biggest percentage movements within the market that day. Now you know how I am able to find hot stocks. Robinhood does the work for me. Can I use other stock scanners or more sophisticated stock screeners? YES! But, then I am adding more work for myself and I want to keep things very simple because I want to show you that you don't need a bunch of computer screens or a bunch of subscriptions to a host of expensive trading alert services to make some nice weekly cash. But, if you like to add some of that stuff it's OK because it doesn't hurt it only helps you trade better.

And just in case someone wants to argue that list is no good, as of this writing that list has brought me a stock I've traded at least four times over the past two weeks. With each day trade profiting me at least a hundred dollars with one of those trades profiting five hundred dollars in about 5 or 10 minutes. I've also watched VinFast, a company that manufactures electric cars (Stock Ticker: VFS) on that list go from a stock price of $11.61 to $82.30. And yes, I wanted to hop on that train and grab some of those profits but my strategy is day trading options and when VinFast was squeezing up making those moves upward it didn't have options available to trade. So I had to stand on the side and watch. Anyway, enough rambling, that's how I find the stocks I want to trade. Wait, I almost forgot to tell you. Once you find a stock on that list that you like, add it to your own watch list so if it ever has more price movements you know about it by looking at your list.

How do I select my strike prices?

Another feature I like about the Robinhood trading platform is how it displays the options chain for stocks. I can clearly see the current price of the stock and the at the money strike prices and the out of the money strike prices. Now here's where my strategy differs from other options day traders. Traders who trade options trade options for the leverage and the time value. Let me explain what I mean. Let's say we have a stock whose ticker is XYZ and its current share price is $100 per share. If you only have $1000 of buying power available in your account to trade with you'll only be able to get 10 shares ($1000 divided by $100/share equals 10 shares). But if you buy one option contract of XYZ company because each option contract controls one hundred shares, buying one contract gets you one hundred shares. Now let's see the power of leverage.

In our first example we were only able to purchase 10 shares of XYZ stock and if the stock price of XYZ went from $100 to $101 per share. That's a one dollar increase. Take the one dollar increase and Multiply it by how many shares you own, which in this case is only 10 shares. You would make $10.00 ($1x10 shares = $10). Looking at the second example you would make $100 because option contracts control 100 shares ($1x100 = $100). Your $1000 gave you more leverage with the option contract.

The other part I mentioned is the time value component of options. All options contracts come with an expiration date. This gives traders some breathing room in case the stock doesn't move in their directional favor immediately. As long as the option contract hasn't expired the contract has value and the trader can still make some profits. Understanding that you could imagine a lot of traders are buying contracts with far out expiration dates to give themselves a sort of buffer and the underlying stock some breathing room to move in their direction.

Here's where my strategy differs. Why? I buy options contracts very close to expiration. Why do I do that? Because I'm day trading the contracts and I'm not looking for much time value. Secondly, shorter expiration dates also means cheaper contracts which works well If you only have $1000 available to trade with. The caveat to this is when you buy options contracts with very little time to expiration, the Greek called Theta, which is the Greek that defines how much value your contract loses daily. And normally, option contracts with short expiration have higher thetas which eat away at the value of your contract. This is why I don't look to hold these kinds of contracts long-term or overnight. These are intraday trades...in and out and on to the next set-up. If all this talk about the Greeks is a little confusing don't worry, in a later section I'm going to explain them in detail.

Pay very close attention to this next section:

Back in 2016 when I first started learning about day trading I learned it from Ross Cameron, a very successful day trader himself. If you never heard of Ross, his small account day trading story is a great one. He took $583 and turned it into $100,000 in 45 days. How do I know he did that? I watched him do it literally with my own eyes. I was a part of his chat room learning day trading and I watched all the trades while I was in my house trying to follow him trade for trade. Of course I was a newbie and tooooo slow getting in and out of positions. But one of the biggest takeaways I got during that season of learning is this: **if you are going to succeed at day trading THE PRICE YOU ENTER THE TRADE MATTERS A LOT**. When I was trading with Ross he might enter the trade 15 to 20 cents earlier than I did because of how fast he was and if the underlying stock price only moved 0.30 to 0.50 cents many times he walked away with profits while I took a loss because of my bad entry price point.

I want to stress this because I have been able profit from day trading options because of the entry points I choose to get in on. Here lies another reason I like the Robinhood trading platform. When you open up a stock's option chain in the Robinhood app directly under the strike prices are the breakeven marks. What this simply means for those who do not understand is this is the share price the current stock price has to get to in order for you to break even and not take a loss if you were to exercise your option to buy the shares of this stock. See S-3 Fig 5. You have to remember that option's contracts come with right to exercise, which means if your strike price is $5.00 and the current share price is $25.00, by you holding the option contract you get the right to buy 100 shares of that stock for $5.00/share instead of the current price of $25.00 instantly adding equity to your portfolio. Most option traders wont have the capital or buying power to exercise their option contract right so they just want to profit from the increase in value of the contract itself. Ill explain this in the next section.

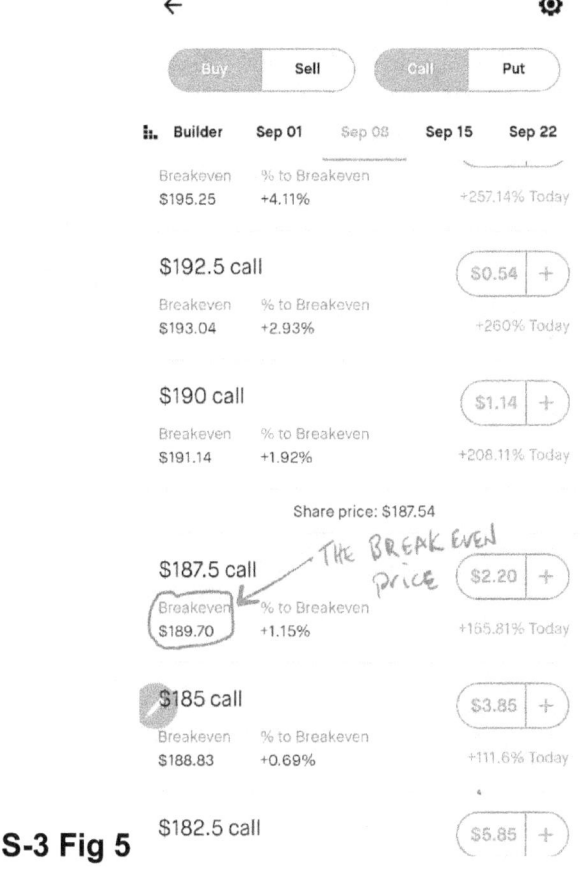

S-3 Fig 5

Let's take a look at a real world example for clarity purposes. Currently Apple is trading at $187.55. (See S -3 Fig 6 below) I'm writing this on August 28, 2023. If we look at the September 8th expiration contracts you can see the 182.50 call strike price, the $180.00 call strike price and the $177.50 call strike price. Looking at the breakeven prices of each of those strike prices, which contract would I buy? Remember, the current share price is $187.55. Did you guess the $177.50

call strike then you are absolutely correct. Why? Because at that entry point the Apple share price only has to move 0.90 cents in my favor before I breakeven on this trade and can exercise my right. Whereas with the $180.00 call strike Apple price has to move $1.35 cents before I break even and with the $182.50 call strike Apple price has to move $2.24 cents before I'm breaking even.

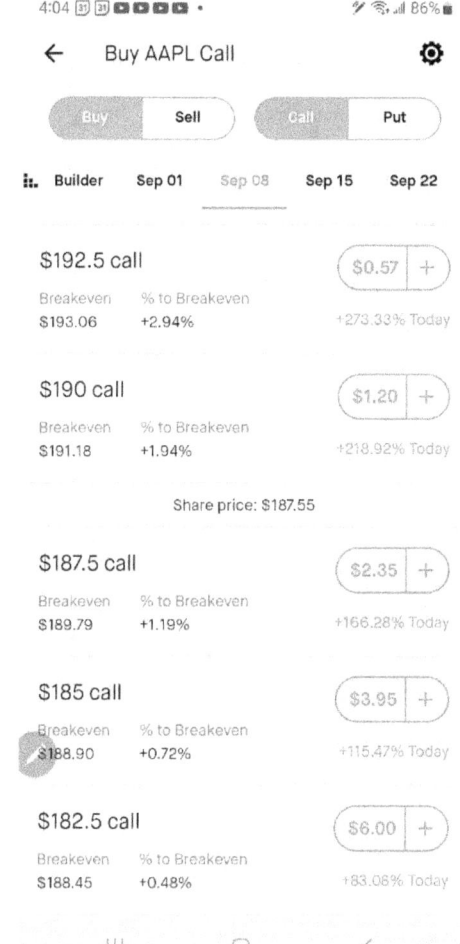

S -3 Fig 6

Buying those call strikes with breakeven prices close to current share price may cost me more money but that's OK because I'm looking for profits early when I enter trades and successful trading is my end goal. But again, this is for those who are looking to exercise their right to own the share at their option's contract strike price.

And just in case you didn't notice, another bonus of this strategy is if the stock doesn't immediately go in my directional favor I still have a few days before the contract expires for the stock to eventually go in my favor as long as it doesn't fall too far down against me hitting my max loss. Then I have no option but to drop the trade and look for my next set up the next day.

SECTION FOUR: UNDERSTANDING THE GREEKS

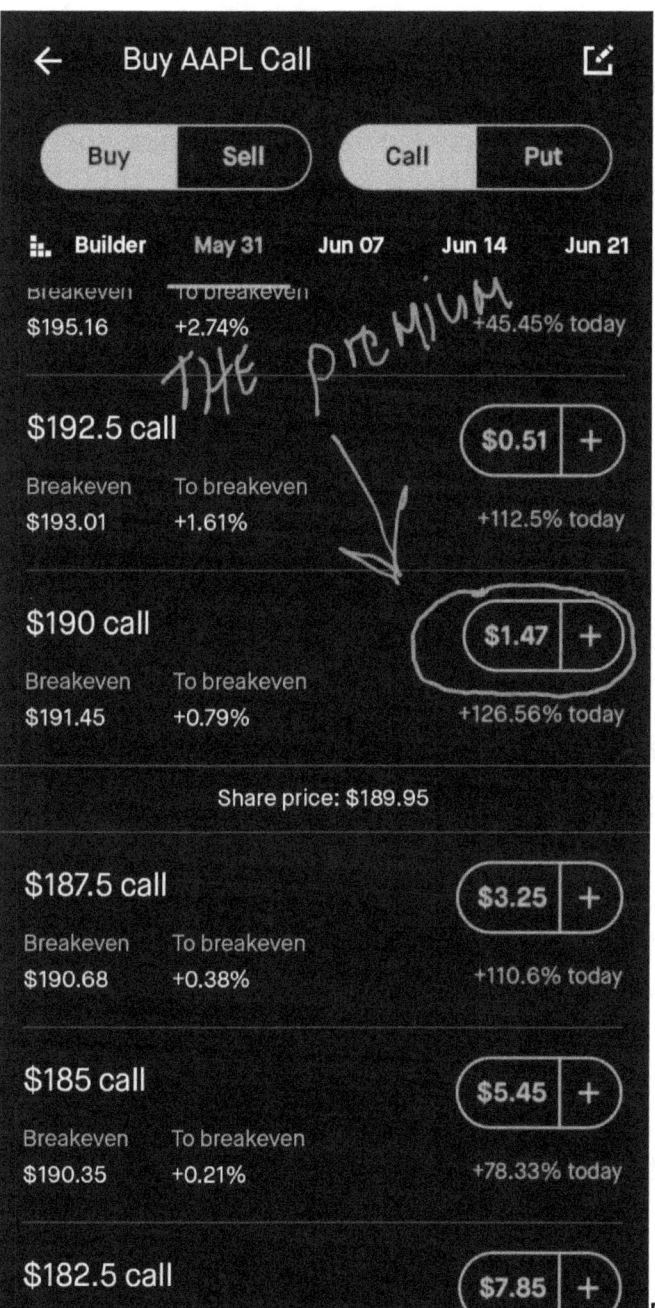

Buy AAPL Call

| Buy | **Sell** | | **Call** | Put |

Builder May 31 Jun 07 Jun 14 Jun 21

THE premium

Breakeven To breakeven
$195.16 +2.74% +45.45% today

$192.5 call

Breakeven To breakeven
$193.01 +1.61% $0.51 +

+112.5% today

$190 call

Breakeven To breakeven
$191.45 +0.79% $1.47 +

+126.56% today

Share price: $189.95

$187.5 call

Breakeven To breakeven
$190.68 +0.38% $3.25 +

+110.6% today

$185 call

Breakeven To breakeven
$190.35 +0.21% $5.45 +

+78.33% today

$182.5 call $7.85 +

Fig 4-1

In the previous section I talked about exercising your option's contract right but mentioned that most option traders wont have the buying power of capital to exercise their right so when they trade options they are looking to profit from the increase value of the contract. So here's how that works and more importantly how it works with my strategy. All options contracts come with a cost to purchase them and this cost is called the premium. Looking at the Fig 4-1 the option contract with a strike price of 190 is $1.47. So if you were to purchase this contract you'd pay $1.47 x 100 which is $147.00. Remember option's contract controls 100 shares so whenever you see a premium you must multiply it buy 100 and you will arrive at your cost for that particular contract. So how does a option trader make money just off the contract? Here's where THE GREEKS come in.

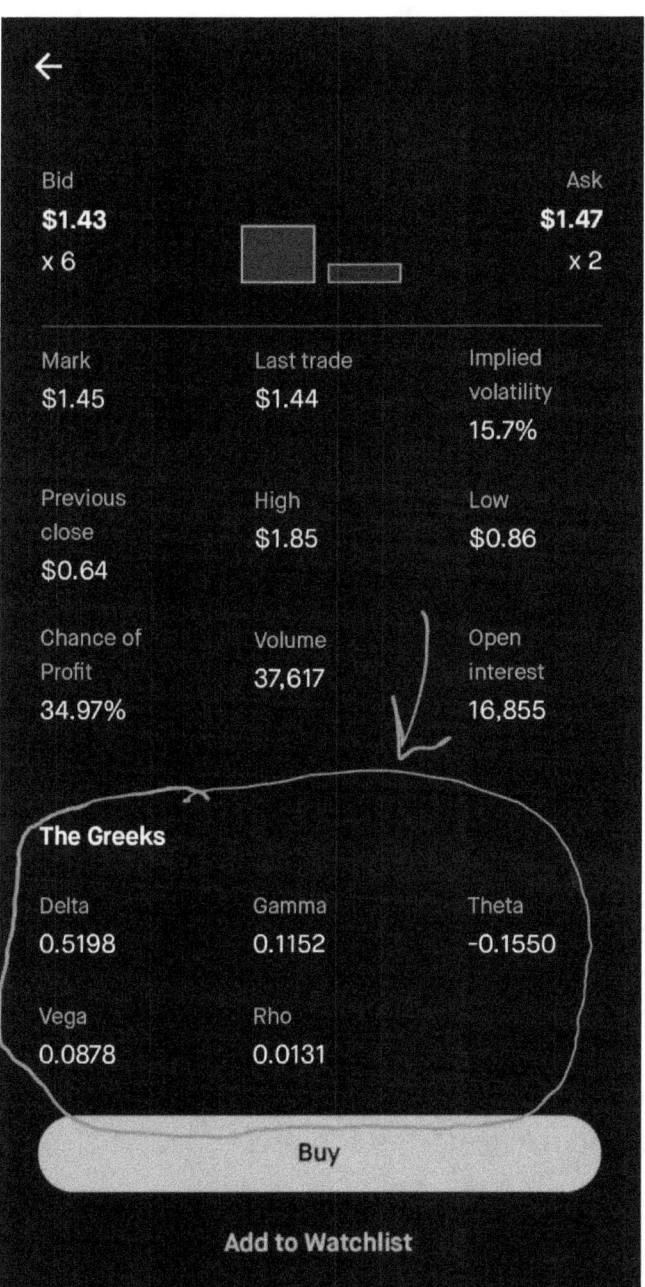

Bid
$1.43
x 6

Ask
$1.47
x 2

Mark	Last trade	Implied
$1.45	$1.44	volatility
		15.7%

Previous	High	Low
close	$1.85	$0.86
$0.64		

Chance of	Volume	Open
Profit	37,617	interest
34.97%		16,855

The Greeks

Delta	Gamma	Theta
0.5198	0.1152	-0.1550

Vega	Rho
0.0878	0.0131

Buy

Add to Watchlist

Fig 4-2

When I click on that contract and look towards the bottom of my screen I'll see the Greeks. There's Delta, Gamma, Theta, Vega, and Rho. Though they all matter the main ones you must be concerned with are Delta and Theta. In this example it shows that Delta is 0.5198 which means that for every $1 increase your option contract premium will increase by $0.51cents (I cut off 98 to make the math more simple). So if Apple share price goes from 189 to 190 and you hold this option contract you'll make $51.00 for every dollar increase ($0.51 x 100 shares = $51.00) and just in case you got too happy if Apple share price goes down from 189 to 188 you lose $51.00. So the higher your Delta the more money you make or lose depending on the share price movements. And vice versa in terms a lower delta. This is why when using my strategy you want to buy options contracts deep in the money with high delta and enter the trade as the stock is beginning to squeeze up or bouncing off of its support. This will allow for immediate profits and quick resolution

Now, Theta plays the role of decreasing your contract value also known as time decay in the options contract world. Traders who plan on holding their contracts overnight, swing trades or long-term must pay attention to this Greek. Theta is the rate the contract will decrease everyday as the contract is moving towards expiration. When trading my strategy Theta is a super villan because we are buying very short expiration Theta is very high and eats away at value of our contracts fast so it's important we get in, get out and take profit with us. In this example Theta is -0.1550 which means our contract will lose approximately $0.15 daily as we move closer to expiration.

Gamma. This Greek determines the rate at which your Delta increases or decreases. In this example our gamma is 0.1152 which mean for every $1.00 increase pr decrease in share price the delta will increase/decrease by $0.11.

Vega is the Greek that determines how much a options price change and implied volatility changes. So in our example Vega is 0.0878 which means for every 1% increase or decrease in implied volatility the option price will increase or decrease $0.08 contingent upon the directional move of the underlying share price.

Finally we have Rho. This Greek measures an expected rate of change of an options based on increases or decreases in current market interest rates

The Precise Point Where I Decide To Take a Trade

What I'm going to teach you here really can not be taught because it comes from being within and trading the markets daily. Once you've been doing it long enough you'll see a stock squeezing up and within your gut you will know it's time to buy in. It's sort of like knowing when it's going to rain outside. You necessarily don't need a meteorologist to tell you when it's going to rain. You can look up outside at the clouds forming and feel the wind speed picking up and that gives you that intuitive feeling of knowing it's about to rain. So you either find shelter or if you have to be outside you dress accordingly and bring your umbrella. Well the same is true when day trading. You'll look at the price movements of a stock and the dramatic increase in volume and the dramatic increase in volatility gives you the feeling that this stock is making big moves and if I want to catch some of the upward swing for profits I better hurry up and buy in. Again, learning this will come in time. This is the secret sauce to making money day trading options. Simply knowing when it's time to buy in.

SECTION FIVE: WORKING WITHIN THE PATTERN DAY TRADING RULE

How do I get around the nasty little pattern day trade rule? My simple answer is this, I don't. I learned years ago from somewhere that the rule was set in place to keep eager uninformed and money-hungry people from financial ruin because as I stated earlier in this book, day trading can cause you to lose lots of money. So this rule helps to prevent that. Having said that, understanding that you only have three day trades within a five day rolling period will make you become more careful on which day trades you take.

Now, the only four strategies I'll encourage if you want to trade a little more than the 3 day trades are these. The first one is the best one because it allows you trade as much as you want as long as you have settled cash in the account. This type of account is called a cash account and you can open one of these accounts at any broker you choose to trade with. In fact, some brokers allow you to change a margin account into a cash account as long as there are no current positions being held in the margin account. So, if you deposit $3000 into your cash account, you can take 3, $1000 trades in a single day or 6, $500 trades in a single day or 12, $250 trades in a single day. In nutshell, long as you haven't traded your entire $3000, you can trade that day. Once you have traded all of your settled cash you cannot trade anymore until the cash settles again which will take one business day. So if you traded on Monday, your money will be available again on Tuesday as long as you were trading options contracts because options contracts take one business day to settle.

The second strategy is tough if you don't have money laying around you could just put into the stock market. But if you do and you have at least $25,000 then just like that you can day trade as much as you like just as long as you keep your account balance above $25k. The third way is more simple and geared towards us little guys with small accounts, just open another trading account on another platform other than Robinhood and that will give three more day trades totaling six. The final strategy I call the *overnight continuation hold*. This strategy works best when you have been trading at least four to six months (not a newbie) and you kind of have a good understanding of how the stocks you've been watching move. I say that because when you see a stock squeezing up and you are familiar with how it moves price-wise but you don't have any more day trades left and let's say it's 12 noon and the middle of the trading day. First, you don't jump into that trade because you won't be able to get out without breaking the pattern day trading rule and 12 noon to 4pm is a lot of exposure risk and the stock could reverse between that time causing you to pull your hair out. What you do is you watch the stock for the rest of the trading day to see if it holds its price levels or continues to squeeze up. If so, you can take the trade around 3:30 pm or 3:45 pm closing your exposure time to 15 minutes before closing bell and hold the stock overnight nullifying it being a day trade and hopefully the stock continues to squeeze up overnight and by morning exit the trade taking your profits. Just know the stock could reverse overnight and open up at a lower price than what it closed at. Just depends on the particular stock. Also, never do the overnight continuation hold if the stock has an earnings announcement after the market closes. Stocks can jump up many points or fall many points after earnings and you don't want to be holding a stock position and it's going against you during the earnings call.

Bonus:

My personal trading stats from right before this book went to print: Out of the 7 weeks I only had one week where I didn't profit. The purpose of this is to show I'm not fabricating. I really do day trade and make money weekly. I highly suggest that you also track your trading stats because like Dr. Benjamin Hardy says "What you measure you tend to get better at."

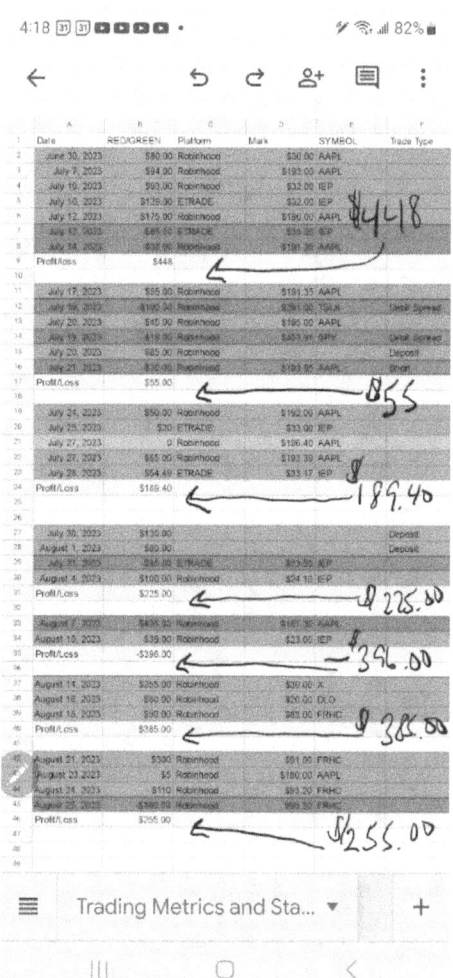

Date	RED/GREEN	Platform	Mark	SYMBOL	Trade Type
June 30, 2023	$80.00	Robinhood	$50.00	AAPL	
July 7, 2023	$94.00	Robinhood	$193.00	AAPL	
July 10, 2023	$93.00	Robinhood	$32.00	IEP	
July 10, 2023	$135.00	ETRADE	$32.00	IEP	
July 12, 2023	$175.00	Robinhood	$190.00	AAPL	
July 12, 2023	$65.00	ETRADE	$33.00	IEP	
July 14, 2023	$32.00	Robinhood	$191.00	AAPL	
Profit/Loss	$448				
July 17, 2023	$55.00	Robinhood	$191.33	AAPL	
July 19, 2023	$100.00	Robinhood	$361.00	TQUA	Debit Spread
July 20, 2023	$45.00	Robinhood	$190.00	AAPL	
July 19, 2023	$10.00	Robinhood	$353.00	SPY	Debit Spread
July 20, 2023	$85.00	Robinhood			Deposit
July 21, 2023	$30.00	Robinhood	$193.95	AAPL	Short
Profit/Loss	$55.00				
July 24, 2023	$50.00	Robinhood	$192.00	AAPL	
July 25, 2023	$20.00	ETRADE	$33.00	IEP	
July 27, 2023	0	Robinhood	$186.40	AAPL	
July 27, 2023	$65.00	Robinhood	$193.30	AAPL	
July 28, 2023	$54.40	ETRADE	$33.17	IEP	
Profit/Loss	$185.40				
July 30, 2023	$130.00				Deposit
August 1, 2023	$80.00				Deposit
July 31, 2023	$35.00	ETRADE	$33.55	IEP	
August 4, 2023	$100.00	Robinhood	$24.10	IEP	
Profit/Loss	$225.00				
August 7, 2023	$435.00	Robinhood	$185.30	AAPL	
August 10, 2023	$39.00	Robinhood	$23.00	IEP	
Profit/Loss	-$396.00				
August 14, 2023	$265.00	Robinhood	$30.00	X	
August 18, 2023	$80.00	Robinhood	$20.00	DLO	
August 18, 2023	$90.00	Robinhood	$85.00	FRHC	
Profit/Loss	$385.00				
August 21, 2023	$300	Robinhood	$91.00	FRHC	
August 23, 2023	$5	Robinhood	$180.00	AAPL	
August 24, 2023	$110	Robinhood	$93.20	FRHC	
August 25, 2023	$300.00	Robinhood	$99.55	FRHC	
Profit/Loss	$255.00				

Handwritten annotations: $448, 855, $189.40, $225.00, -$396.00, $385.00, $255.00

≡   Trading Metrics and Sta... ▼   +

||| ◯   ‹

Stay blessed my friends.

www.ingramcontent.com/pod-product-compliance
Lightning Source LLC
Chambersburg PA
CBHW062259290526
45794CB00006B/2624